Exposing Autism

Finding the New Faces of Neurodiversity

By

Gregory C. Bowen

TABLE OF CONTENTS

INTRODUCTION

Autism is seen today as a complex formative inability portrayed by hardships with correspondence, communication, and conduct. With side effects clear right off the bat throughout everyday life, specialists and clinicians concur that no single variable is capable. They find mental imbalance's starting points in a mix of hereditary qualities, nervous system science, and natural chemistry. The exact reasons for mental imbalance, and its formative components, stay as baffling as could be expected.

Autism is constantly addressed as a riddle. It influences various people in an unexpected way. So striking is the variety — a few people can't involve language or care for themselves while others arc profoundly keen, verbal, and independent — that mental imbalance presently runs over a wide range of mental, social, and close to home capacities. Autism Spectrum Disorder, or ASD, has as of late entered the jargon of conclusion and handicap to a limited extent since chemical imbalance might end up being a bound together condition.

Later on, it is conceivable that we will allude to mental imbalance in the plural: autisms.

Autism's authentic vocation has been brief and questionable. The term was presented during the mid 20th hundred years and showed up in clinical writing during the 1940s, most broadly in a 1943 article by Leo Kanner. At that point, chemical imbalance was not really a natural word, not to mention a clinical condition or finding. Somewhere in the range of 1900 and 1943, case narratives and reports on autism-like circumstances, including hospitalism, showed up in Europe as well as in the United States. The terms youth schizophrenia and adolescence psychosis were utilized to portray chemical imbalance in kids until something like 1970, prompting a lot of disarray about what these terms implied and how to separate them.

Preceding the 1960s, psychogenesis was the predominant hypothesis about mental imbalance. Its key clarification was that mental imbalance was incited by genuinely oppressive guardians — especially moms — who could be altogether ignorant about the harm they were doing to their youngsters.

At the point when those moms kept the affection vital for typical turn of events, babies and small kids answered by withdrawing into mental imbalance, which offered a sanctuary from parental antagonism at the unreasonable cost of extremist partition from every single human connection. Psychogenesis started losing validity during the 1960s and another logical worldview focused on science instead of brain research made strides, energized by neuroscientific examination and parent activism. "Chemical imbalance" showed up in psychiatry's symptomatic book of scriptures, the DSM, in its initial 1952 release, yet it was not recorded there as an autonomous disorder until 1980. Autism's definition has never been steady. Its demonstrative models have forever been in transition.

Public familiarity with mental imbalance has filled emphatically in ongoing a long time for some reasons. Natural psychiatry influentially reclassified different dysfunctional behaviors and profound issues as formative incapacities, moving consideration away from the relational domain and moving it definitively toward the cerebrum. Journals by Temple Grandin, Donna Williams, and other mentally unbalanced people were distributed during the 1980s and 1990s, giving surprising bits of knowledge into the emotional experience of chemical imbalance interestingly.

In the last part of the 1990s, widely acclaimed debates about whether youth immunizations were embroiled in chemical imbalance scared guardians and stressed general wellbeing authorities, sustaining against inoculation developments that have created episodes of measles all around the world. Most as of late, banters about "neurodiversity" have entered mainstream society and online assets have duplicated for individuals living "on the range."

Autism is more natural and apparent today in the United States than ever previously, yet we actually have hardly any familiarity with its set of experiences.

CHAPTER 1

What's truly autism?

Autism syndrome disorder(ASD) is a complex neurodevelopmental problem by and large appearing in the initial not many long stretches of life and having a tendency to persevere into pre-adulthood and adulthood. It can be referred to as "chemical imbalance". It is portrayed by deficiencies in correspondence and social connection and limited, monotonous examples of conduct, interests, and exercises. It is a problem with multifactorial etiology. It is the most notable of a few unavoidable formative problems (PDD) analyzed which start in youth and go on over the course of life, influencing practically every part of life en route. While mentally unbalanced people groups' mental (thinking and language) and interactive abilities are commonly formatively deferred contrasted with their companions, their engine (development) abilities foster in a more typical design.
Chemical imbalance is a deep rooted condition that influences how an individual learns and communicates with others and their environmental

factors all through their lives (from youth to adulthood).

Each autistic kid and youngster has various qualities, interests and capacities. No two medically introverted kids are something very similar. Yet, there are a few normal qualities of autism. Explicit social association, correspondence and conduct shortages should be available before the determination of chemical imbalance is proper. However all individuals with autism show similar explicit examples of debilitations, the seriousness of these impedances differ from one case to another, for certain individuals exhibiting somewhat gentle weaknesses and others exhibiting extreme hindrances.

From an early age, youngsters with autism show an essential trouble in appropriately situating towards others and in handling social and non-verbal types of correspondence, for example, eye to eye connection and look. For example, a normal newborn child is by and large receptive to grown-up parental figure looks and will copy those articulations. Assuming that a parent grins at a newborn child, that baby is probably going to grin back. This isn't true with newborn children with autism, who frequently come up short on capacity to see the value in faces or socially conveyed sentiments.

Kids with autism are additionally commonly deferred (now and again harshly so) in their improvement of communication in language and conversational abilities.

People with chemical imbalance likewise will generally show odd and socially improper ways of behaving. They much of the time act with indifference with regards to other people, and stay separated from their environmental factors. Many fixate or focus on specific items or on specific points they see as expressly intriguing. They might demand discussing a point they find entrancing in any event, when others around them are not intrigued. They might carry on odd generalized developments and motions. They might exhibit a serious requirement for request and equivalence as to their current circumstance, and respond with fits when their valued request is upset. As a rule, individuals with autism's absence of social mindfulness makes it troublesome or inconceivable for them to explore through regular circumstances effectively.

Side effects of mental imbalance are absent from birth. Most youngsters with autism seem to grow regularly during the main year of life.
Side effects of chemical imbalance become clear somewhere in the range of eighteen and three years of life. A little less than half of cases are analyzed by age three. Mental imbalance is an equivalent open door sickness; No specific race or social class will in general get it more regularly than another. In any case, it is undeniably more probable (four to multiple times more probable) to happen in guys than it is in females. When laid out, medically introverted side effects go on into adulthood. The side effects range in seriousness (across people) from generally gentle to extreme and weakening. In everything except gentle cases, autism impedes common turn of events and makes it troublesome or unimaginable for impacted grown-ups to live and work freely. However mediation can't switch the course of autism, it can bring about side effect improvement and a more noteworthy capacity for freedom. For mediation to find lasting success, in any case, it should be conveyed right off the bat in the formative cycle, soon after the analysis of mental imbalance is first made.

Chemical imbalance gives off an impression of being happening more much of the time than was the situation before. The predominance (pace of event) of autism has ascended from five in each 10,000 during the 1990's to one in each one-hundred and 66 of every 2005. The numbers are evening out and appear to be on the downfall, however the ascent in the quantity of instances of chemical imbalance is faltering. There is not a great explanation for the sensational increment, however mindfulness might assume a critical part. A lot more kids who have gentle types of mental imbalance might be being analyzed essentially in light of the fact that guardians and pediatricians have become more acquainted with the side effects of mental imbalance.

CHAPTER 2

Understanding autism masking.

What is autism masking?

Masking, which is likewise called veiling or redressing, is a social step by step process for surviving. It is an interactive ability that people with mental imbalance take on in group environments in which non- autistic individuals anticipate non-medically introverted conduct. Covering can appear to be unique from one individual to another, it tends to be portrayed as a fundamental three-stage model of the interaction: inspiration, veiling, and results.

How it looks will fluctuate from one individual to another, yet concealing can incorporate ways of behaving like these:

- constraining or faking eye to eye connection during discussions
- mirroring grins and other looks
- mirroring signals
- stowing away or limiting individual interests
- fostering a collection of practiced reactions to questions

- prearranging discussions
- pushing through extraordinary tangible uneasiness including clearly commotions
- camouflaging stimming ways of behaving (concealing a wiggling foot or exchanging a favored development for one that is more subtle)

Individuals might veil mental imbalance for various reasons, for example,

- having a real sense of security and keeping away disgrace
- Keeping away from abuse or harassing
- Prevailing at work
- Drawing in a better half
- Making companions and other social associations
- fitting in or feeling of having a place

Concealing your identity is an awkward and debilitating experience. For the overwhelming majority medically introverted individuals, that experience is an everyday reality.
Masking starts when a neurodivergent individual perceives that something significant depends on being seen as neurotypical. Perhaps it's

companionship. Perhaps it's an open position. Perhaps it's for my own wellbeing.
Ladies are specialists at chemical imbalance veiling, specialists say. Society requests social collaborations between young ladies, where young men are permitted to foster a maverick persona. The additional time young ladies enjoy with their neurotypical peers, the more purported "miniature dismissals" they experience, including:

- Curious looks. Young ladies who stim are much of the time given open gazes from their friends.
- Giggling. Examining a most loved point finally can end with ridiculing laughs.
- Separation. Young ladies who are different aren't welcome to gatherings or get-togethers.

As these affronts add up, young ladies figure out how to constrict their way of behaving. They quit doing things that others remark on, and they might try and find a good example to duplicate. They burn through a large portion of their school hours figuring out how to be very much like their companions while stripping away anything that makes them even marginally unique.

As these young ladies develop into grown-ups, their propensities become dug in. They're seasoned veterans of impersonating companions and flying just underneath the radar.

Young ladies are so great at chemical imbalance veiling(autism masking) that they even concealed their side effects from analysts. As of late, says Autism Speaks, did analysts find that ladies are on the range. Today, analysts are finding out increasingly more about how ladies cover mental imbalance side effects to dodge discovery.
Where the full range of neurodiversity isn't perceived or invited, autistic individuals frequently want to introduce or perform social ways of behaving that are considered neurotypical. Certain individuals may likewise feel they need to stow away neurodiverse ways of behaving to be acknowledged.
Many individuals expect that medically introverted individuals have no friendly or mindfulness, yet periodically this fantasy is only that: a legend.

Anything that inspires an autistic individual might feel they should conceal contrasts or significantly impact the manner in which they normally act. These mentally unbalanced grown-ups most usually veil their chemical imbalance to find a place with non-autistic individuals. They need to stay away from others' harassing and negative responses towards them. Moreover, they may likewise cover their autism since they are worried about how they go over to others when they don't change their way of behaving. They feel their living or work space doesn't endure backing or regard neurodivergent [autistic] ways of behaving.

Life structures of concealing autism

Autism concealing is an arising research region that spotlights on figuring out the cognizant or oblivious concealment of normal medically introverted reactions and reception of choices across a scope of spaces. It is proposed that veiling might connect with pessimistic results for medically introverted individuals, including late/missed determination, psychological well-being issues, burnout, and suicidality.

This makes it fundamental to comprehend what veiling is, and why it happens. In this applied examination, we propose that concealing is an obvious reaction to the deficiency story and going with shame that has been created around chemical imbalance. We frame how old style social hypothesis (i.eSocial character hypothesis) can assist us with understanding how and why individuals mask by arranging covering in the social setting in which it creates. We draw upon the writing on shame and minimization to look at how concealing could converge with various parts of character (e.g., orientation). That's what we contend in spite of the fact that covering could contribute toward variations in finding, we genuinely must n't force orientation standards and generalizations by partner veiling with a "female mental imbalance aggregate." Finally we give proposals to future exploration, focusing on the requirement for expanded comprehension of the various ways that chemical imbalance might introduce in various individuals (e.g., incorporating and externalizing) and multifacetedness. We propose that veiling is inspected through a socio formative focal point, considering factors that contribute toward the underlying improvement of the cover and that drive its support.

Cost of masking

Masking/veiling might be normal where there's little help for neurodiverse individuals, or where individuals on the chemical imbalance range are under direct danger. In any case, while veiling might have specific advantages, it's essential to take note that there are huge expenses.

Time invested learning neurotypical ways of behaving is energy not put resources into different sorts of self-improvement. What's more, the work used to duplicate neurotypical collaborations can rapidly prompt social over-burden.
However, advocates say covering can deny networks the valuable chance to be aware and acknowledge individuals as they truly are. Individuals with chemical imbalance don't have the right to stow away and untruth and veil their longings. They should be acknowledged as they are. That's what concealing forestalls.
Here are a portion of the impacts of standard masking:

- Stress and tension. Analysts observed that pressure and tension were higher in individuals who regularly veiled mentally unbalanced qualities, contrasted with the people who utilized covering on rare occasions.

- Sorrow. In 2018,111 mentally unbalanced grown-ups were consulted, finding that the individuals who detailed covering their medically introverted characteristics had side effects of despondency and felt unaccepted by individuals in their social circle.
- Depletion. Veiling consumes colossal measures of energy. Ladies who utilized veiling to fulfill neurotypical principles said they felt depleted by the consistent exertion.
- Deferred distinguishing proof of autism. Certain individuals are so effective with veiling that their chemical imbalance isn't recognized until they are a lot more established. That postponement can prompt psychological well-being issues since individuals don't get the help or understanding they need.
- Loss of character. Certain individuals who veil their character, interests, and qualities wind up feeling that they never again know who they truly are. Some have said

concealing feels like self-double-crossing; others have said covering causes them to feel they're beguiling others.
- Chance of autistic burnout. At the point when individuals drive themselves to act in manners that don't feel bona fide, the outcome can be a staggering sensation of over-burden, at times called mentally unbalanced burnout.

Covering might require a lengthy time of calm withdrawal and recuperation.
Expanded hazard of self-destructive contemplations. As of late, drawn out covering has been connected to "lifetime suicidality." The review was moderately little (160 understudies) and involved fundamentally ladies (89.6 percent). Nonetheless, it showed that veiling prompted feeling like a weight, which thus prompted more self-destructive considerations throughout the span that could only be described as epic.

CHAPTER 3

Reexamining Autism

Regardless of whether expected, this pervasive driving explanation emits the impression of an objective clinical determination. Since the actual analysis is consequently enriched with this face legitimacy, it is extraordinarily tested by quite a few people. In any case, maybe we ought to vigorously examine and challenge it. Maybe we want to constantly continue posing the extreme inquiries in regards to what legitimacy it can profess to have and all the more significantly, whether one or many better definitions could exist.

After some time, the scene of autism has changed decisively - from a once limited to now wide definition, from being uncommon to now being normal in the populace, from something concentrated on principally in youth to now being seen across the life expectancy, from something discrete to now something a smidgen more layered, from being one "chemical imbalance" to many "autisms," from unadulterated to complex, and from "jumble" to "neurodiversity".

With this change over the long haul, it ought to be expected that we do some reconsidering on the idea and challenge ourselves regarding our suppositions. Numerous in the field have proactively started that conversation and the exchange ought to go on until we arrive at an upheaval or change in outlook that drastically changes what is happening to further develop in regions that are as of now vigorously missing, and which are most significant given the targets of the local area and the field. In this viewpoint piece, we will contribute one drop into this expanse of "reexamining mental imbalance" from a zoomed-out point of view expected to essentially advance fresh reasoning on the subject. On the off chance that we are to "reconsider autism," we ought to zoom out and not make numerous suspicions about what ought to be taken as reality and begin posing exceptionally fundamental inquiries about the historical backdrop of the name, what the analytic mark was/was not expected for, and whether our ongoing spotlight on certain highlights as opposed to others might have misled us. We finish up with a relationship about the idea of "trees" that might be valuable in delineating comparative sorts of reasoning and how we could reconsider the subject.

In pushing ahead, remembering your steps might be valuable. A first way we can reexamine autism is just to glance back at its set of experiences. For the individuals who have quite recently entered the field, this might be a troublesome undertaking, however there are a few vital references here which we believe are fundamental perusing on the point. We won't go through every one of the subtleties here. In any case, to sum up one example that set of experiences has shown us up to this point, that's what it is "autism" is definitely not a static idea after some time, nor is it liable to be some goal "thing" out in nature ready to be found and better comprehended. Rather, "what is autism" has changed extensively after some time and will probably keep on developing as we push ahead. This idea of progress in the analytic idea over the long run is essential to know about, on the grounds that we shouldn't wait around accepting the ongoing idea is fundamentally more right than past originations. Thoughts, for example, "prototypical chemical imbalance" caught by Mottron and partners close by weaning impact sizes over the course of the years might uphold the possibility that a past origination of mental imbalance was more effective. In any case, the sheer reality that the actual idea is non-stationarity ought to train us to be profoundly suspicious of any current or past origination and any face legitimacy that the conclusion might be verifiably supplied with upon first look. One way we could possibly assess whether the ongoing circumstance is addressing our requirements ought to be to address what the finding is great for, yet in addition what the conclusion isn't great for. Unquestionably, we would have no desire to hurl out the finding for all the great it does in certifiable conditions, however we ought to likewise not fanatically clutch it and oppose change when we can all concur with its numerous deficiencies. Recognizing the non-stationarity of the demonstrative idea itself, by means of a glance back at history, ought to be the most important phase in having the option to give up and consider the chance of better approaches to describe chemical imbalance that fits the ongoing climate and requirements of the local area and field.

Among the numerous striking key changes over the course of autism that could be remarked on, here we disconnect one explicit change point that we accept is profoundly pertinent for highlighting a significant change in the populace scene of chemical imbalance.

In 1987, the DSM standards transformed from a monothetic (all models should be met) DSM-III to a polythetic (not all measures need be met) DSM-III-R rules. One of the most sensational impacts of this monothetic-to-polythetic shift was the sidelining of early language issues as a center and fundamental component. Before this specific moment, powerful people key to the development of DSM-III measures, like Michael Rutter, had proposed that early language issues were a vital element of chemical imbalance. Nonetheless, with the rise of Asperger's unique contextual analyses to the English talking world, outstanding people, for example, Lorna Wing were persuasive in contending that the idea of autism be more extensive than that of Kanner's and DSM-III, especially concerning whether early language issues were fundamental. Wing likewise presented the idea of the side effect set of three (e.g., social, correspondence, and RRB) and the thought of a "range" to additionally grow how social-correspondence troubles could appear in changed kinds of people (e.g., unapproachable, detached, and dynamic yet odd). Wing's impact for this more extensive view were significant variables in the DSM-III-R changes and to a polythetic unwinding which likewise made early language issues unnecessary. These progressions are logically significant for providing us with a more extensive and more complete perspective on the heterogeneous way that social-open issues can emerge in various people. Notwithstanding, the effect of the change in regards to the unimportant idea of early language issues can't be put into words. This change considerably reshaped how the autism populace could be conceptualized - from once being a greater part of people with significant scholarly and early language issues, to these days mirroring a greater part of medically introverted people without such issues. The effect of combining as one such person is as yet an unmistakable and current clinical issue. For instance, as perceived by a new Lancet commission, the mark right now being used (combining as one a wide range of people) doesn't imply the differential requirement for administrations and backing that the most significantly impacted people require.

CHAPTER 4

Building an autistic life

Over the course of life, each individual faces difficulties, snags and troubles that they should survive. The capacity to return through misfortune is called versatility. Strength includes managing difficulties in a proactive manner which helps fabricate certainty and dominance in defeating hardships. Having the option to do so upholds self-improvement, psychological wellness, and adds to good identity worth and confidence.

Autistic individuals have various degrees of debilitation, which can go from gentle side effects to an extreme inability. How much fundamental abilities preparing required will shift in light of the impacted person's necessities. By and large, a great many people with autism will require a level of treatment to address language, correspondence and social communication issues to have a more straightforward progress into standard society. Flexibility is a self-repeating expertise in light of the fact that once an individual has effectively dealt with a difficult circumstance, they'll have good expectations about their capacity to defeat tough spots. As certainty develops, resilience does as well. Individuals with autism face explicit difficulties that can cause mishaps around sensations of certainty and self-esteem. Living in a non-autistic world can be overpowering and terrifying. An absence of facilities can prompt tension, stress and burnout. Conveying one's necessities effectively can be troublesome, especially on the off chance that there are not suitable backings set up to have the option to do as such. An absence of consistency can be distressing; new exercises can set off implosions or closures.

Without strength, medically introverted individuals can find life progressively testing, will be unable to adapt to new things or changes, and might need to pull out from social circumstances. Building strength right off the bat in life can assist a kid with feeling sure to take on new difficulties and succeed.

Life Skills and Autism

What Are Life Skills?

For individuals with autism, mastering fundamental abilities is crucial for increment freedom at home, at school and locally. By presenting these abilities early and building block by block, individuals with chemical imbalance gain the apparatuses that will permit the person in question to increment confidence and lead to more bliss in all everyday issues.

Fundamental abilities are once in a while alluded to as free living abilities or day to day living abilities. Fundamental abilities incorporate taking care of oneself exercises, cooking, cashing the executives, shopping, room association and transportation. These abilities are mastered after some time, starting at home early in life and growing further all through pre-adulthood and adulthood.

Our fundamental abilities systems and thoughts will assist our local area with beginning and give apparatuses to help keep advancing through the progress from school to grown-up life.

Certain everyday routine abilities are important for day to day experiencing. Contingent fair and square of disability, an individual with chemical imbalance might require fundamental abilities help with the accompanying regions:

- Discourse and language help
- Correspondence and interactive abilities preparing
- Instructions to follow bearings
- Potty preparation
- Dressing freely
- Cooking and housekeeping abilities for free residing
- Work preparing

Learning an extensive variety of fundamental abilities that apply to numerous everyday issues is basic. It is additionally vital to incorporate leader capability abilities or thinking abilities, for example, arranging, arranging, focusing on and dynamic connected with every fundamental ability being educated. Greater classifications of fundamental abilities include:

- Wellbeing and security

- Vocation way and work
- Self-assurance/support
- Peer connections, socialization and social correspondence
- Local area cooperation and individual accounting
- Transportation
- Relaxation/diversion
- Home residing abilities

How to teach life skills

Each individual with autism is unique, so the fundamental abilities that will be instructed, and the speed that they are educated, will fluctuate from one individual to another. For instance, one youthful grown-up with autism may eventually have the option to live on their own with very little, if any, outside help, while another may require support and administrations 24 hours every day, 7 days per week. Beginning to foster fundamental abilities to the best of a kid's capacity early in life will have an effect as they age.

There are perpetual fundamental abilities to realize which will be educated and rehearsed at home, school, and locally. A great many people with chemical imbalance benefit from clear, active guidance in fundamental abilities that will assist them with expanding freedom.

Daily routine Skills classes or free experiencing programs are well known ways of mastering these abilities and are normally driven by an instructor or specialist. Fundamental abilities preparing ought to happen in common habitats where the abilities being educated relate straightforwardly to the sort of climate the individual is going to reside in and use them. This implies mastering cooking abilities in a kitchen, or acquiring clothing abilities in a laundromat.

CHAPTER 5

Fostering an autistic relationship

Throughout recent years, an ever increasing number of individuals have asked themselves how they can establish a chemical imbalance/autism accommodating climate. Planners have expounded on planning mental imbalance agreeable structures and families have renovated rooms to give positive tactile encounters.

Clear from standing by listening to individuals have an autistic range condition that they can encounter the world contrastingly to other people. This can be both weakening and enabling. In establishing an autistic accommodating climate, we should attempt to diminish the adverse consequences of tangible contrasts and upgrade the beneficial outcomes.
The troubles related with social cooperation, correspondence and creative mind are the absolute most difficult parts of having chemical imbalance. This set of three disabilities makes the 'glass container' in which I live. The glass container makes it truly challenging to associate with individuals. It is a decent figurative depiction for: not fitting in,

social tension, being an onlooker not a member, feeling desolate in any event, when around others, having various interests...
Connections have forever been truly challenging for myself and actually I can't meet the 'neurotypical' assumptions that a great many people have. For instance, the sort, recurrence and span of mingling that many individuals do - especially toward the beginning of a relationship - isn't workable for me to stay aware of. I could do without getting things done in the nights, meeting someone else's loved ones is upsetting, I could do without chatting on the telephone, I want an exceptionally huge measure of alone time and security, and I don't look for exercises that are beyond my typical daily schedule (even extremely 'typical' things, for example, going to a bar or a bar, or going to the film or a workmanship display cause me gigantic measures of tension).

As may be obvious, there are various troubles that the two of us need to fight with.
The way into an effective relationship is correspondence. As a matter of fact, I have discovered that perhaps the best thing in a potential accomplice is great relational abilities - or possibly

an eagerness to be a superior communicator. I as of now find correspondence exceptionally hard so I should be with somebody who finds correspondence simple and agreeable. They should be receptive and patient and comprehend that verbal discussion is hard for me, especially while I'm feeling worried. Composing or attracting or composing to one another - regardless of whether not done continuously - can be truly powerful.

An individual who needs to have a relationship with me should comprehend that my routine is basic to my psychological prosperity. Frequently this implies I will be unyielding and unbending about the things we do and the times we do them however in the event that somebody can fit in around the daily schedule (and we're both content with the game plan) then, at that point, we will both wind up appreciating each other's conversation significantly more. Early arrangement for different things beyond the standard is significant and can permit us to do these things with as little pressure as could really be expected, as opposed to pass up them by and large. For instance, to take a quick trip and see a specific film at the film, we will design together:

The most agreeable chance to go (work day mornings will quite often be calmest).
How we will go there (cycling or strolling are dependably best over open vehicles).
What we will do after the film has finished (for the most part, we go straight home).
Fostering a relationship is most likely more troublesome than keeping up with it. It requires a ton of work to foster a beginning 'level' of closeness (for example fellowship) in light of the fact that to get to know each other, I must be focused on finding out about the other individual and investing energy with them. This responsibility can be hard, in light of the fact that my regular needs in life are: separated from everyone else's time, routine and my exceptional interest.

Until the other individual comprehends what autism is and - in particular - what it means for me (which can truly occur through time and experience), it's simple for them to uncertainty my degree of interest and obligation to them, making them leave relationship prospects.

Keeping a relationship requires difficult work and exertion from the two individuals yet when the two individuals know one another alright (side interests, dependability, reliability, day to day plans, even such words and sort of language we use, and so forth), there is less strain to 'perform' and on second thought of being not able to live up to ridiculous assumptions, we can meet genuine ones.

The way into an enduring, cheerful relationship for the two individuals is to lay out 'decides' so every individual understands what they can and can't anticipate from each other and thus won't be disheartened in the event that they are not met. For instance, assuming my accomplice has let me know that watching football is essential to him, I will adapt better in the event that he decides to watch a match as opposed to seeing me for our ordinary 'routine time'. In the event that he had not told me from the outset that football was essential to him, I'd find it hard to adapt to his choice because of my powerful urge for things to constantly be something very similar, paying little mind to outside factors. For my purposes, the benefits of seeing somcone having the option to associate with somebody and have the amazing chance to emerge from the previously mentioned glass container and consequently I feel less alone on the planet.

I like that we can do 'typical' things together, like talking, strolling the canine, or having some tea, without getting exhausted. For his purposes, he has somebody extremely clear and really exceptionally keen on finding out about his encounters, contemplations and sentiments. He knows where he is with me. For the two of us, our coexistence is unsurprising, unwinding, and consoling.

CHAPTER 6

Making a neurodiverse world

We are living in a period of expanded neurodiversity and mindfulness about ADHD, Dyslexia, Autism, and other neurological states. Truth be told, one out of eight individuals are considered neurodiverse however less than 50% know it. Neurodiversity will in general be high energy, out of the container masterminds, succeed in an emergency, and be striking issue solvers, however exploring the cutting edge work environment can be a test. Not exclusively is planning space to be comprehensive the proper thing to do, there is a convincing business case for it too. Space today needs to mirror the different cosmetics of associations to put all in a good position.

Before we dig further on neurodiversity, it is essential to initially comprehend the way things are characterized. The word neurodiversity alludes to the variety, everything being equal, however it is in many cases utilized with regards to ASD, as well as other neurological or formative circumstances like ADHD or learning handicaps.

The thought individuals having a scope of various sorts of mind, incorporating those with and without mental imbalance, ought to be viewed as a component of ordinary human existence. The idea of neurodiversity is frequently used to allude to the chemical imbalance range, and a few definitions might incorporate learning handicaps as well as emotional wellness conditions.

It is assessed that somewhere in the range of 30% to 40% of the populace falls under the classification of "neurodiverse," and society is making progress to be more comprehensive to people who fall under this umbrella. Organizations in each area, as well as instructive establishments, are starting to understand the advantages of making facilities for a neurodiverse crowd.

The neurodiversity development arose during the 1990s, intending to expand acknowledgment and incorporation surprisingly while embracing neurological contrasts. Through web-based stages, an ever increasing number of medically introverted individuals had the option to interface and structure a self-support development. The idea of neurodiversity isn't new. Judy Singer, an Australian humanist on the mental imbalance range, started involving the term during the 1990s.

Vocalists dismissed the possibility that individuals with chemical imbalance are debilitated. Her view was that their minds simply work contrastingly . She set forth energy to advance balance and consideration of "neurological minorities."

A few activists in the mentally unbalanced local area and past hug the term. They and others have involved it to diminish disgrace and advance consideration in schools and in the working environment.

While it is fundamentally a civil rights development, neurodiversity examination and schooling is progressively significant in how clinicians view and address specific handicaps and neurological circumstances.

The 21st century is tied in with driving maintainable development and carrying advancement to all that organizations do. There is sufficient and more information to recommend that individuals on the autism range can prod advancement and get alternate points of view.

Considering this foundation and as we progress increasingly more towards a computerized and innovative subordinate world, in my view it checks out to employ neurodiverse people.

Employing neurodiverse competitors isn't tied in with making special cases. It is tied in with employment for ability. A couple of months prior, our association surveyed neurodiverse competitors and after a thorough three-step process we made offers to the chosen up-and-comers. We intend to recruit more neurodiverse ability and guarantee they feel included. Neurodiverse people are frequently mechanically slanted and conscientious. These people can be persistent and steadfast laborers. Their sensible and direct reasoning can prompt cycle upgrades that can thus increment efficiency. We accept that similarly as we employ individuals with expert abilities in specific capabilities, recruiting neurodiverse people for their abilities is the shrewd thing to do.

Large, significant change can truly begin with little and straightforward advances. Start by having discussions with HR, the business and obviously variety and consideration champions, pioneers. Enroll neurodiverse applicants, who have the right stuff required for the jobs, deliberately. Standardize discussions about individuals who are unique and worth individuals who think in an unexpected way. This will drive development and all the more significantly, make major areas of strength for having a place in individuals.

In under 30 years of coordinated action, the chemical imbalance privileges part of the neurodiversity development has advanced from the periphery to the edge of the foundation. As it has developed from an essentially socio-social extension to a functioning piece of a cross-handicap freedoms alliance, the neurodiversity development has moved expanding center toward what it goes against, yet additionally what it upholds. Expanding commitment on viable issues from the harmony among wellbeing and independence to conceptive and nurturing privileges have made the limits of activists' positions more clear and offered down to earth help in regions, for example, through tool stash and various book presses possessed by mentally unbalanced and other neurodivergent individuals. Autistic individuals (and our associations) have become progressively included and perceived in chemical imbalance backing, for instance we have been counseled (close by parent-drove associations) on issues from Hillary Clinton's 2016 official mission to a mentally unbalanced Sesame Street character, creating results that satisfied the mental imbalance local area for the most part.

We are totally conceived in an unexpected way, raised in an unexpected way. Our reasoning varies from one another. Our uniqueness acquires fluctuated points of view and creative thoughts and this is the same for neurodiverse individuals. Driving genuine change, constructing a world that works better can begin basically by including various voices and regarding contrasts.

CONCLUSION

This book has endeavored to report the activities of driving autistic activists in neurodiversity development, covering the set of experiences when it has gone through various waves in its turn of events, yet not beyond any good time to draw in many pursuers from the nations where it has become most established. It has likewise looked to make sense of the ideas of neurodiversity and the convictions and work of neurodiversity development, drawing in with studies when misconceptions wait. "Neurodiversity-light" has chemical imbalance culture (embracing a portion of the way of talking of the development yet not really carrying out the standards: maybe principally to obliviousness yet additionally co-choice of the development's fortifying force(e.g. changing an association's name however not its practices. The development has gained extraordinary headway and has started to enter governmental issues, yet except if the development further blends in a more extensive alliance in additional districts of the globe, its effect on battling the developing in a worldwide cutthroat economy might be restricted.

Future books and works of grant and activism might additionally reveal insight into the ongoing status of the development past its beginnings (past mental imbalance and quite a ways past chiefly anglophone nations), and dismantle ways ahead for aiding neurodivergent individuals get the help and regard we want.

www.ingramcontent.com/pod-product-compliance
Lightning Source LLC
LaVergne TN
LVHW050011170826
845677LV00023B/3903